CH00905618

# ONCE UPON A DREAM

## Manchester Dream Weavers

Edited By Warren Arthur

First published in Great Britain in 2017 by:

Young Writers
Remus House
Coltsfoot Drive
Peterborough
PE2 9BF
Telephone: 01733 890066
Website: www.youngwriters.co.uk

# FOREWORD

Welcome Reader, to 'Once Upon A Dream –
Manchester Dream Weavers'.

Do you dare to dream?

For Young Writers' latest poetry competition, we asked our writers
to dig deep into their imagination and create a poem that paints
a picture of what they dream of.

The result is this collection of fantastic poetic verse that covers a
whole host of different topics. Snuggle up all comfy and let your
mind fly away with the fairies to explore the sweet joy of candy
lands, join in with a game of fantasy football, or you may even
catch a glimpse of a unicorn or another mythical creature. This
collection has a poem to suit everyone.

Whereas the majority of our writers chose to stick to a free verse
style, others gave themselves the challenge of other techniques
such as acrostics and rhyming couplets.

There was a great response to this competition which is always
nice to see, and the standard of entries was excellent. Therefore
I'd like to say congratulations to the winner in this book, *Sophie
Njai*, for their amazing poem, and a big thank you to
everyone else who entered.

Warren Arthur

# CONTENTS

## St Margaret Mary's RC Primary School

| | |
|---|---|
| Alfie Atkinson (8) | 69 |
| Joshua Solomon (10) | 70 |
| Mili Gibson (11) | 71 |
| Layla O'Malley (7) | 72 |
| Charlie Lomas (7) | 73 |
| Savannah-Rose Gethin (10) | 74 |
| Elliah Caine (10) | 75 |
| Ruby Bates-Clarke (9) | 76 |
| Cain Wildbure (10) | 77 |
| Tomisin Comfort Olutayo (10) | 78 |
| Kevin Kusmierek (11) | 79 |
| Jessica Fairchild (8) | 80 |
| Alex Lomas (11) | 81 |
| Mia Nolan (8) | 82 |
| Emma Jenkins-Meehan (7) | 83 |
| Caitlin Marie Burrows (9) | 84 |
| Luca Daniel Robertson (10) | 85 |
| Angel Owa (8) | 86 |
| Remi Smith (9) | 87 |
| Lacey Inman (11) | 88 |
| Gabriel Downes (11) | 89 |
| Jennifer Otame (8) | 90 |
| Mikayla Ocheja (10) | 91 |
| Joel Lynch (10) | 92 |
| Brooke Taylor (7) | 93 |
| Olivia Blackwell (9) | 94 |
| Ella-Rose Taylor-Dolan (8) | 95 |
| Jennifer Dayo Ogunjobi (10) | 96 |
| Jayden Barnes (8) | 97 |
| Louis (9) | 98 |
| Shondrella Gachoka (11) | 99 |
| Thomas Hulston (7) | 100 |
| Iliana Dimitropoulou (10) | 101 |
| Joseph Tattersall (9) | 102 |
| Erin Bennett (10) | 103 |
| Liam Mcculloch (10) | 104 |
| Liberty Thompson (10) | 105 |
| Liam Kearney (8) | 106 |
| Thomas Leggat (8) | 107 |
| Sienna Kelly (8) | 108 |
| George Francis Partington (9) | 109 |
| Tom Fauguel (10) | 110 |
| Wiktoria Pietras (8) | 111 |
| Alex Cooke (9) | 112 |
| Katie Ann Dean (10) | 113 |
| Bailey Reese Downes (8) | 114 |
| Michael-Joe Creilly (10) | 115 |
| Hayden Scott Lindley (8) | 116 |
| Oliver Anthony Steven Newman (10) | 117 |
| Libbie Gerzsei (10) | 118 |
| Aiden Leggat (10) | 119 |
| Leighton Woodlock (9) | 120 |
| Lois Bennett (8) | 121 |
| Max Middleton (10) | 122 |
| Laykia Bell (9) | 123 |
| Joseph Bailey (8) | 124 |
| Daniel Trotter (10) | 125 |
| Mia Pandolfo (10) | 126 |
| Scola Wakomo (7) | 127 |
| Benjamin Blackwell (11) | 128 |
| Kiera Doyle (10) | 129 |

## St Mary's RC Primary School

| | |
|---|---|
| Paul Connolly (9) | 130 |
| Samuel Kane | 131 |
| Leon Lebeter (9) | 132 |
| Samantha Sheldon (8) | 133 |
| Michael Sunmola | 134 |
| Grace Wakefield Chinnery (9) | 135 |
| Sofia Da Silva (9) | 136 |
| Kiera Fortune (9) | 137 |
| Nancy Wilson | 138 |
| Ruairi Nisbet | 139 |
| Freya Grace Rothwell (9) | 140 |
| Dave Anil (9) | 141 |
| Vesta Balseviciute (9) | 142 |
| Munachi Unagha (9) | 143 |
| Jazmyne-Antonia Devon Corbishley (8) | 144 |
| Kaven Shepley (9) | 145 |
| Ben Kahraman (9) | 146 |

## St Michael's CE Primary School

| | |
|---|---|
| Alex Cardus (6) | 147 |
| Charlotte Suzanne Redfern (7) | 148 |
| Nathaniel Jacobs (7) | 149 |
| Violetta Farrington (7) | 150 |
| Carter Burgess (7) | 151 |
| Will David Thompson (7) | 152 |
| Leo-Alan Sparkes (6) | 153 |
| Archie Ryan Kilroy (7) | 154 |
| Evan Lewis Vines (7) | 155 |
| Sienna Hannah Hostey (7) | 156 |
| Georgina Davies (7) | 157 |

# THE POEMS

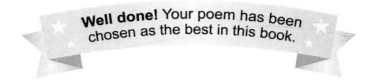

# Candylandia

Staring at the sparkly night as I stare at the glittery
stardust
I spot a star sign that looks like Taurus!
Gummy bears spill out of a unicorn's mouth
As a gingerbread man is building a gingerbread house!
I rule Candylandia as an astonishing queen,
Known as beautiful as a unicorn so it seems.
Joyfully I swim in the chocolate ocean like a supple
mermaid
With a colossal chocolate dragon
Soaring through the pink cotton candy clouds
Whilst the radiant, primrose sun beams
I ride on the Pegasus, as on the top of my voice,
I scream!

**Sophie Njai (10)**
St James CE Primary School

1

# What Treasure?

I shut my eyes to find quite a surprise
I'm walking up to my new boarding school
After the summer in the pool
Up the stairs I come
There's new buildings but only some
I look at my papers which says I'm in the sixth house
I count 1, 2, 3, 4, 5, 6 and I walk up as quiet as a mouse
I knock on the door, *creak!*
The door opens and I realise the ceiling has a leak
'Hello,' I shouted, 'anybody there?'
I dropped my bags and turned around to see a lady
with long hair.
Suddenly, she walks through me
And then I see
A man who shakes my hand firmly
He shows me the house and says there's treasure there
'What treasure?' I ask and he says,
'The treasure is buried in the house.'
'Who buried it?' I ask.
'The ghost lady of the house.'
And then backs away
Then suddenly I wake up
What did I dream of today?

**Ruqqaiya Kabir (10)**
Chapel Street Primary School

# My Dream

I dream to be a unicorn flying over rainbows and
clouds,
I dream to be an astronaut going to space and
exploring planets
that nobody has ever explored
I dream to be a pirate sailing the sevens seas and
hunting for gold.
I dream to be a clown juggling balls and riding in a
unicycle
Made out of pretzel and shooting whipped cream.
I dream to be a footballer, training and scoring goals.
I dream to be a dancer dancing on stage, live and
jumping everywhere.
After a long time of dreaming
I go back to sleep and I wander off to a magical land
of sleeping.

**Nour Youness Alharess (10)**
Chapel Street Primary School

# Flying To School

I got into bed
With a very sore head
I fell fast asleep
After counting eight sheep

I woke up the next day
To my little brother wanting to play
I got myself dressed
Although I didn't look my best

It was eight twenty
I'd already eaten plenty
I ran out the door
I was going to be late for sure

I started to run
It wasn't very fun
Until my feet felt very light
It gave me quite a fright

When I realised I was off the ground
I started to look around
I was in the sky
I think I was starting to fly

Was that Superman?
There went Peter Pan!
Was that a dragon
Sitting in a station wagon?
I think I'm late for school
I'm gonna look a fool
Didn't I just go past a bear?

**Amara Karena Gonzalez Manning (10)**
Chapel Street Primary School

# Gymnastics

When I do gymnastics
I feel fantastic
It makes me smile
And it doesn't make me feel vile
I do it all day
Even in the month of May.

I always compete
And everything I do I complete
I always feel nervous
Especially when I go on beam
And when I'm on it I never lean
And I always win
And every time I do, I get better and better.

One day I get a letter
Saying I get to be a professional gymnast
And I get to go to the Olympics
When I get there I swing on bars
After that I eat some Mars.

When I get my score
It isn't poor
It is great!
Just like my mate.

And I win!
I feel as bright as the sun
Then I am a famous professional gymnast!

**Aleena Fatima (9)**
Chapel Street Primary School

# My Planet Dream

I shoot up in a rocket, piercing a hole in our ozone,
As I look back I see it being sewn up again all neat and clear,
Mars bellows over the rattle of the engine,
'Hello drone!'
*Crash!* Asteroids colliding in front of me, fear strikes into my heart,
I charge through the Milky Way and hear a mighty groan.

*Creak! Thud! Drop!* my rocket sounds like the noises in wood,
I frantically swim out,
No helmet, nothing, I have to get back, I should,
I find a nearby planet with sprouts in the sea and growing trout
What should I do?

I float around in nothing, just stars
They illuminate the air,
Banging and booming, fizzing and exploding,
A star explosion takes place in a distant galaxy,
I look back with such a great care,
Earth is like a speck of dust circling an orange continuously,

I flip and turn,
And hear my 'go-back' device beep
I now need to be careful so I don't burn,
My asteroids arrive like a jeep.

Flames from the sun jump and dance, melting
Mercury and warming Earth
As I arrive back to our world
I realise something with no disagreement
I've just seen a birth of my planet Dreament.

I'll come back soon,
It is actually true,
But maybe I'll bring some cheese from the moon,
Nobody knows you, my dear Dreament, I won't give a
clue.

**Rebeka Szentgyorgyi (10)**
Flixton Junior School

# Transforming Into Lego Man

**L** aunching into the playroom I jumped to the floor,

**E** ager to play with my brand-new Lego

**G** laring straight at the see-through figure behind the door,

**O** h that figure looks like a digger now,

**M** iaow, purred the cat slurping at the bowl of water,

**A** choo! I sneezed, putting snot all over the figure,

**N** ow I cleaned it up just before I touched it
- *whoosh!* - I turned into a Lego figure

**T** rying to turn back into a kid again, I felt like I was a constipated child,

**R** oaring for the cat to help me (but of course it couldn't understand)

**A** nnoyed sitting on a Lego sofa which actually felt quite snug,

**N** ow running into my new and improved Lego house,

**S** ulking that I might get trodden on by the cat,

**F** linging myself into the house, I raced up the stairs

**O** n the top floor feeling a breeze which was the cat's breath,

**R** ocking back and forth because I was in front of the radiator,

**M** oaning that I wanted to change back into a child,

**I** now found the Lego figure, then I changed back,

**N** ow transforming back into a child again and
throwing the Lego in the bin,
**G** etting onto the sofa, resting and
watching Lego Justice League on the television.

## Luke Starczewski (10)

Flixton Junior School

# The Dumb Detective

There was a stupid person,
He was as thick as could be,
He also had a spy glass so that he could see,
He was a dumb detective,
The worst in the land,
He was so dumb you could put his brain in your hand,
His name was Jonny.

The only problem was he lived next to the Queen,
His house compared to hers was as small as a bean,
She had statues of hands,
How greedy!
A golden necklace,
Pearls, rings,
Ooh, they must have
Lots of dosh
How very posh.

He was a clumsy man,
And he fell over,
Ah, the loner,
*Thud! Thud!*
Huh, that second one wasn't him,
So he got a pin as sharp as him.

Setting off,
He opened the door,
And sneaked inside as loud as a boar...
He found a giant,
It was a house!
He was a mouse!
Then he called guards,
They ran up the hall,
Red suits gleaming bright,
Lanterns hanging from a height.

Jonny,
Oh no, it was a dream,
He could have met Her Royal Majesty. (Gutted)

**Matthew Gardner (9)**
Flixton Junior School

# The Autumnal Baby Dragon

The two deep pools in his eyes,
They reflected off the moon in the dark, black night.

His crimson-tinged scales touched the autumn hue,
A new pair of wings, erupted like an angry volcano,
Filled with hot, bubbling goo.

A fire lit in his mouth and squirted out like dancing
ribbons,
Bubbling and boogeying, it was,
It was like food covered in pigeons.

The wings beat as fast as lightning,
It looked kind of scared, almost frightened.

He started to lift from the ground to a hover,
I didn't chase after it, it did not want to be bothered.

Its fire warmed me as I was chilled to the bone,
Then it left me all alone.

I dreamt of the dragon, till the sky was black,
I thought of the dragon but it never came back.

I thought up a plan to lure it back home,
Problem was, it flew out my zone.

I woke up in bed, realising it was a dream,
Turns out that dragons are not real,
Well now I need to get clean.

**Annabelle Hustwitt (10)**
Flixton Junior School

# A Bad Dream

A bad dream is my greatest fright,
*Bang!*
Goes a blaring, penetrating knock on the door,
*Thud!*
Goes a footstep on a defective tile
Dark and gloomy is the night.

A bad dream is my greatest fright,
My house is made out of zombies and graves
I live on my own, in the countryside,
Graves shudder and stare at you as if alive,
Zombies start to invade my house,
Their brains hanging for their noses,
Blood cascades down the flesh of their torsos,
Dark and gloomy is the night.

A bad dream is my greatest fright.
*Thud!*
A clown is in my sight
Its alabaster face is as white as the clouds in the sky,
The manic grin spreads across his pallid, anaemic face
Dark and gloomy is the night

A bad dream is my greatest fright,
Half of Harambe's body lies in a tree in the graveyard,
My front garden has a pool of blood,
Ghosts haunt graves,
Dark and gloomy is the night.

**Toby James Maccabe (10)**
Flixton Junior School

# The Night I Saw A Jet Of Light!

It's midnight,
But it doesn't give me a fright,
Then I look out of the window and I see...
But no, it cannot be,
A jet of light in the middle of town,
As bright as the sun,
However, it looks like fun,
So I run downstairs and grab my coat,
Then I open the door and see a billy goat,
'Baaa baaa' it chuckles persistently,
Then I notice its knobbly knee,
We reach the wizard
As he's creating a lizard,
His hair is gold and green,
A very humorous thing to be seen,
He turns the lights off without a switch,
Then he gives his remarkable wand a twitch,
Incredibly, they turn back on,
He has not once lost this fantastic flow,
He is amazing, he's superior, he's enthralling,
Not one of his spells are appalling!
Shooting spells pink and yellow,
He must be quite an old fellow,

So then I say,
'I think I'll go back to bed,'
Then I wake up from such an amusing adventure,
I'm getting ready for tomorrow night's adventure!

**Isaac Fitzsimmons (9)**
Flixton Junior School

# My Dream Come True!

Once upon a time, a crisp silhouette of a thick, black, blanket
Lay gentle and soft on the rigid land,
As the clock struck 12, dings danced around the streets,
Quickly imprinting themselves in those humans' ears,
The cat was pouncing on its meek prey,
As the house scurried away, laughing underneath thy clock.

Over to thy west, the beautiful radiance of a quiet landscape,
A quiet place of a quiet life... lies over an old house,
And to thy last, birds sang gently about their favourite charming tune
In a lullaby like song or a tune,
Unlike at blazing noon.
Where supporters sang an uprising song about their team

As it is slowly getting brighter
*Howl, howl*
The grey wolf sings like an opera singer.

In this world pigs do fly with angel like wings
A world that doesn't need queens or kings,

This world is a dream land where evil is extinct
At night, light doesn't shine but it is silent and calm
And in the crazy dangerous day, I fly!

**George Tinsley (11)**
Flixton Junior School

# Zombies Ground

The zombies were as ugly as a living rotten lion
Blood of fresh victims
Streamed out of hundreds of mouths
Creating a river of blood.

Footsteps banged on the ground
Shattering like an earthquake, the zombies
approached the house.

The zombies, which were as ugly as anything in the
entire universe,
Charged at the deserted house

The wood that barred the window prevented
them from getting in
The house burped out half a dozen grenades onto the
house's grounds
In the distance there was a dog barking at the legions
of zombies
Their leader, John Ordinary, led the charge.

The bang of gunshots filled the air
The shotgun which had loads of air in the bullets
Smashed and sent 20 or 25 zombies flying
They got crushed into the bushes.

The Red Devils flew from Mount Zorb and were now weakening the zombies
They both charged at the house heroically and valiantly.

## Cameron Wilson (10)
Flixton Junior School

# From The Roof Of My House

From the roof of my house,
I can see people as small as ants,
Their hats,
Their coats,
Are all easy to see.

From the roof of my house,
I can see all the shops,
Their signs,
Their bright colours
Are all easy to see.

From the roof of my house,
I can see people's back gardens,
Their rows of flowers
Their football nets,
Are so easy to see.

From the roof of my house,
I can see the land and sea,
The roads,
The boats,
Are so easy to see.

From the roof of my house,
I can see my back garden,
My tree house sitting all alone,
My flowers sitting in the pots,
Are impossible to miss.

From the roof my house,
It is a wonderful view,
The sun going down,
Like an egg yolk drizzling into a cup
Shows me it's time for bed.

**Richard Bond (10)**
Flixton Junior School

# Future Me

I opened my eyes to find myself
In a house with filth in the door frames
With creepy crawlies scattered all over the windows
And the floor was covered in waste.

I glimpsed to my side
And I got spooked as I noticed man on the couch
*Bang!* The shock hit me faster than a bullet
I realised the man was actually me but in the future.

Every time I looked at my future self,
My brain started to ache,
I wanted to look away
But I couldn't look away, it was just so abnormal.

I tried to distract myself, so my brain didn't ache,
I looked at a piece of paper dancing around,
I glanced at future me but he disappeared.

I ran outside to find him,
But as I started running,
I got transferred to a new dimension,
But then realised it was all a dream.

**Charlie Turner (10)**
Flixton Junior School

# Killer Clown

Thunderclouds appeared and lightening began to strike - what had just happened?
The sun has only just shone,
The wallpaper started ripping down and halted as the last shred has gone,
Its menacing laugh filled the air and it's colourless face was pressed to mine, His sapphire hair was as wavy as a slithering snake as well as fine,
I start to run as fast as I can - down the hallway through the old oak door,
He starts chasing me as soon as I tripped onto the hard grimy floor,
His shoes were as big as canoes so they screeched and squeaked on the floor each step he took,
He cackled his sickening laugh again and shot me a mischievous look,
He thundered towards me, his clothes laughing and wiggling whilst he walked,
The clown took a step closer and then stalked,
Now I was his prey, in despair, I closed my eyes and held my head,
I woke with a start and realised I was safe tucked up in bed.

**Katy Ruff (10)**
Flixton Junior School

# The Flying Traveller

I flew like an eagle, as I saw the country below me,
I flew down, I saw that I was in China,
I saw the dragons and people dancing as I
walked through the city,
Gradually, I floated up to my next destination.

I felt the wind blowing on my face as I zoomed to
Australia,
When I flew down I saw lots of different animals,
Looking around like a cheeky monkey, I saw a couple
of trees,
One tree danced as I walked by.

A zebra went by,
So I hopped on the zebra,
The zebra was a beautiful black and white zebra,
The zebra clip-clopped like a horse as the sunset was
coming,
Then the luminous stars started to glow as the sun
went down,
I immediately fell in love with the animal.

Suddenly, I heard a loud
*Tick, tock, tick, tock,*
Sadly my alarm woke me up.

**Milly Hulme (10)**
Flixton Junior School

# Fairie Gardens

**F** airies dance blissfully in the night sky as the music shouted,

**A** round the fire the fairies stared as the fear pouted,

**I** n the small fairy garden the fairies pause

**R** aging smoke poured out of the minute doors

**I** had always dreamt of such a place

**E** ven my mum had a cute fairy's face.

**G** rasshoppers chasing around the fairy garden

**A** ll the fairies harden

**R** eady for the morning and to turn back to stone

**D** rip the very last unicorn tear parachutes down, down

**E** ven the homes were as camouflaged as a blaring tank

**N** ow for the old rotting manky dirt, you need to get money from the bank

**S** o the next time you see the statue of fairies in somebody's garden, use your imagination to wake the magic.

**Sadie Clephane-Warham (10)**

Flixton Junior School

# The Astracorn

I got to the ship, as colossal as Mount Everest, as
gigantic as can be
*Whoosh, swoosh!* Off I went, beating out into space
Rainbows shone from my unicorn horn
For I was a Hucorn, half human, half unicorn,
My head was furry and sparkly, whilst my body was
a man
Eventually I reached the moon, past noon it was indeed
The moon was larger and the moon was vast.

*Crash! Smash!* I ended up on the moon
I saw Earth, I saw Mars, I saw Jupiter,
I even saw the star humans call the 'Sun'!

As I looked up, I saw many shiny objects,
I even thought I saw one or two smile back at me
The moon was made of cheese,
So I enjoyed my cheese picnic
The moon was no more,
Who would've known the moon would lead to my
doom?

**Toby A J Mcsyrett (10)**
Flixton Junior School

# The Great Kingdom

Peacefully the rising sun burst lights engaging angels,
illuminating the kingdom.
Sweet villagers wake up to a grand castle
looking over the humble sties.
Meanwhile, over in the fabulous mountains
beastly dragons sheltering.
The sky like an ashen of shields.
As after, in the clearing princes battle bloodthirsty
centaurs
to win the heart of a princess.

*Whoosh!*
The wings of a Pegasus soared through
the misty enchanted forest through the misty treetops.
Woodcutters carried life-threatening axes
like executors as their next tree falls to the ground
As the sun set through to the end
the night was cast over the kingdom.
The only sound was the sound of silence
in the great kingdom.

**Jenson Ford Bottomley (10)**
Flixton Junior School

# Secret Door

One day I went to play in the forest nearby,
I could hear the soothing noise of water dash by

The trees dance to the music of the wind
There was an abandoned cottage by the towering hills.

As I went on, there was a glimpse of tiny dancing lights
Which were as small as a speck of dust.

I took out my magnifying glass
There seemed to be little people with wings
Of course they were fairies!

The little people seemed to be leading me somewhere
I looked up and there was a secret door

I had a key for the door, I walked through the door
And woke up!
I wish to be in that beautiful garden again.

**Amber Johnson-Magee (10)**
Flixton Junior School

# The Abandoned House

I am not prepared for this nightmarish adventure,
The unstable, historic abandoned house,
Is known to be haunted.
As nervous as can be, I take small steps towards the doorway,
Terrified, bats fly knocking the torch from my hand.
*Clink! Rattle! Bang!* A tin can rolls across the floor,
Something tells me I'm not alone.

Running, running,
From the distant groan.
I look back a few more times.
It comes closer and closer,
My worst nightmare!
Clowns run from the eerie, sinister house,
Two hands grab me and begin to pull me back,
Aaah! The eyes scowl right into mine, my heart beats rapidly.
I found myself, just then in bed with no harm
It was all a dream!

**Ben Harrison (10)**
Flixton Junior School

# A True Dream

A lion stands before me
A monkey at my side
A massive roar that deafens the land
The monkey drops and dies.

The ground opens up
All I see are orange flames
I close my eyes and think to myself
*Their king will be ashamed.*

A beach facing the ocean
Crashing at the sand
Everything is modern
In the old, sandy land.

Wake up, wake up, it's morning
My eyes open like a sloth
I sit up in the light,
With a yummy hot chocolate froth!

Am I still in a dream?
I ask the person at the side,
It is a very hairy monkey
Of course, it's still night!

I'm now in a colourful rainbow!

**Matthew Kenny (10)**
Flixton Junior School

# Make-Up Island

As fancy as a Georgian woman's face
*Ding, ding,* the clock strikes
And then the pucker of the lipstick bell,
Magnificent eyeshadow roads
And pathways crack as you step on them.
Fantastical blusher brush trees brighten the place up
Mascara brushes are the trees in winter
Lipstick residents patrol around,
Cracking the eyeshadow here and there.

Down the road is the lipgloss swimming pool
Lipstick makes up the houses
It really is a wonderful sight
Beautiful blush flowers dance in the breeze
Lipgloss children shouting in happiness
*Flutter, flutter, flutter* go the mascara butterflies
Alas, my dream is my choice.

**Evie-Mae Jones (10)**
Flixton Junior School

# Terrors At Night

**T** hunderous footsteps
**E** ndlessly shaking like an earthquake
**R** avenous creatures approaching from all directions
**R** ustling leaves dance in the twilight sky
**O** ver the distance wind whistles through the night
**R** aging and roaring, thunder shoots from the sky
**S** woosh! Something sweeps across the ground, ready to seize

**A** fter dark, creatures emerge
**T** ilting trees towering

**N** ever walk alone in this deadly forest
**I** ntense surroundings
**G** hostly moans filling the air
**H** orrors in the trees ready to capture you
**T** errors like in the menacing woods.

**Daniela Loi (10)**
Flixton Junior School

# Ghostly Castle

I was sound asleep when I got into a dream
A massive castle shining from the distance,
When I got closer the shining stopped
There I was, stood in front of the arched door,
I went in.

Suddenly, I saw a black cloaked person
I explored the castle
I saw a pale person in front of me disappear
I was stood terrified,
I ran out of the room and someone appeared...
The ghost appeared, there was a moment of silence
I could hear the dripping of the rain on the roof.
I ran out of the door as fast as Usain Bolt.
And there he was stood looking out of the window.
Then I woke up and realised it was just a dream.

**Jacob Jones (10)**
Flixton Junior School

# The Lily Pad Prom

Fairies dance in the moonlight,
Whilst the frogs sing on the lily pad together,
Elves bring out ginger beer, cherries and lots of other
goodies to have.

Mice and bunnies gather round and join in the fun,
Whilst nightingales sing like children doing a Christmas
carol,
Mythical creatures do a lovely dance,
Whilst the cute, little bunnies prance.

The trees gently sway as the wind blows by,
The fairy queen appears in a glittery cloud,
All the creatures cheer, hooray, hooray, hooray
The woods have little mushroom houses for all the
creatures to live in,
Little ponds dotted around, tiny wooden boats and
little trees.

**Carly Williams (9)**
Flixton Junior School

# A Dragon Ride To Topsy-Turvy Land

Excited, I climb upon the fearsome beast
The tiny trees below us seem to wave bye,
As we take off into the sky
We are flying rapidly through the air,
As fast as an eagle hunting prey
My dragon's blood-red wings are flapping furiously,
As I grip his scaly body.

Suddenly, Topsy-Turvy Land comes into sight
With a sudden swoosh, we land with a fright.
Shocked, I sat with amazement,
As people walk on their hands,
With my mouth open like a goldfish,
I look at green sky and blue grass
My dragon's dancing flames turn blue...
Then I wake up and find myself in bed!

**Esmé Hilton (10)**
Flixton Junior School

# The Rainforest

**R** are species strewn all over
**A** stonishing landscape with trees surrounding wildlife
**I** n the background
**N** ever-ending green expanded to nothingness
**F** lora scattered over the leafy land
**O** paque tree wood as brown as dirt that has
been dug up for centuries
**R** ustle! Explorers thrash down bushes like chainsaws
**E** ternal life has the trees
**S** piral bark waving and dancing in the wind
**T** he rainforest.

**L** and like no monster
**A** stonishing things here and there
**N** ever-ending life
**D** ecorated trees with green and brown.

## Charlie John Gilbert (10)
Flixton Junior School

# A World Of Pure Imagination

The trees are like fluffy coloured clouds
Covering the land
The fish singing their favourite songs,
Happily as a girl on her birthday,
The bears staring at me, eating their marshmallows
*Nom nom nom nom nom...*

I stare at the sky
Feeling like I'm about to cry,
As the doodlefluffs fly high in the sky.

My extraordinary, enormous house
Is made from different-coloured obsidian,
Filled in with stained-glass windows.

The breeze blows the trees as they dance in the wind
As the shiny sun waits to awaken a brand-new day.

**Lois Rhiannon Howells (10)**
Flixton Junior School

# Planet: Theme Park

Race on down to planet: Theme Park,
Travel there on a wondrous, blinding rocket
To a planet of unpredictable fun.
There is a roller coaster which is as fast as a cheetah,
Oh I wish I could go to the never-ending food court
I'd slurp up the milk from the Milky Way
I would drift off to sleep as the bus flies away
And takes me to the other side of the planet.
There are candyfloss roller coasters,
A mountain of candy fun,
And then I carefully walk over to the exit and,
*Bang!*
I'm back at home, safe in bed
I wish I was on planet: Theme Park.
Grrr!

**Alfie David Martin Flynn (10)**
Flixton Junior School

# If Toys Were Alive

If toys were alive, they'd be asleep with you in
your bed,
If toys were alive, they'd pester, plague and irritate you
until you're dead
If your toys were awake, you'd never escape,
You'd be haunted for the rest of your life,
Then you'd just have to strife,
Is it alive?
It would be a nightmare.
Soon you'd see changes to your hair
Your hair would turn as white as alabaster
If this were to happen to you,
Escape the house while you can
Otherwise you'd end up as a dead old man.

## Ethan Chatwood (9)
Flixton Junior School

# The Haunted House

The haunted house just looks at me in anger,
Its windows look like eyes!
*Drip! Drip! Drip!*
You can hear the broken tap...
The house is made out of gooey slime,
The smoke is made out of ashes
From the people he has killed and burnt
His uncomfortable toilets are filled with blood from
5,000 years ago
The house is as creepy as a dark cave filled
with monsters in it...
His library is filled with books about how to kill
innocent animals.
He keeps gruel to eat every single day.
This is the dream that haunts me!

**Inaya Khan (9)**
Flixton Junior School

# Space Chickens

Flowing, intense, nebulae capered like a flame on a
booming bonfire
The resplendent Pegasus and I are climbing higher and
higher
Space is perpetual, never ending
Vibrant galaxies are twisting and bending
Like a roller coaster in a theme park
Space is a thousand lights put together, it is so dark!

*Whoosh!* A glistening trail of ice and rock is left behind
As a shooting star soared through space. Wow! That's
one of a kind
Weird, why are the scorching stars thawing in my face?
Wait a minute, why are chickens in outer space?

**Emily Stewart (10)**
Flixton Junior School

# The Fun House

My friends, where have you gone?
Come, come, we are in the fun house
I walk in to start the fun
The confetti cannon exploded - *bang!*
It's as loud as a lion's roar
My friends slurp their milkshakes but it ends up all over their faces
As I see the big drop, my friends pushed me straight down
Speedily sliding down at 99mph
When I got to the bottom
I see sweets and chocolate walking in a line
Then I eat them for some reason
I can hear my mum... wait, where's the fun house?
Noooo!
It's just a dream.

**Andrew Hollis (10)**
Flixton Junior School

# Flying In Your Dreams!

Soaring through the air like a fast incoming plane,
I found out that I could fly,
A plane roared and growled
Leaving a dancing trail of smoke behind,
As I touched the clouds, they felt like candyfloss,
The birds tweeted, as the rain dropped,
I kept on flying up and down till I saw a mountain in sight,
The sun had shone upon the mountain with its 'beyond big' light
I headed closer and closer,
As the air rushed through my hair and onto my face,
Lightning zapped. It was soon upon me,
But then I realised... it was all a dream.

**Olivia Grace Prideaux-Penny (9)**
Flixton Junior School

# Sunny Evil

It is a nice, sunny day, everyone is happy, everything is happy.
The sun shines down on the beautiful village.
The butterflies are flying, the trees are blowing and everything is fine.
Suddenly, a giant comes out of nowhere.
Everyone screams like a dragon breathing fire.
Silence - it turns dark.
It is as dark as the midnight sky.
The giant roars as loud as thunder and lightning.
*Drip, drip, drip* - the water drips down, down, down.
Everything is pitch-black.
Springing up rapidly, I woke in horror but luckily I am safe in bed.

**Emily Ackerman (10)**
Flixton Junior School

# Nightmare

**N** ightmares, nightmares I detest nightmares
**I** n the dance halls, where the candles flicker
**G** uaranteed
**H** ow, how the walls are closing in today
**T** oday, I don't want to die today, I am still as
young as a child.
**M** y worst nightmares chasing me
**A** clown, a killer clown I really hate them
**R** unning after me as fast as it can, and when it is
about to get me
**E** lated, I'm in my bed safe and sound.

I'm really glad to know it was...
Just a nightmare!

## Molly Scanlan (10)
Flixton Junior School

# Dragons

Peering out the ashy window
Dragons
Mighty creatures
Dangerous creatures
Kind creatures
Kind to me
Only.

Looking out the burnt door
Dragons
Burnt trees shudder
As they pass
Amiable creatures
Sentient to me
Only.

Standing on the ashy street
Dragons,
My burnt house
Peers like a dragon
Harmful creatures,
I help them,
Only.

Jogging across the cobbled road,
Dragons
They take off
Gone,
Forever
*Boom!*

## Eleanor Crowther (10)
Flixton Junior School

# The Living Dead

In the dark, gloomy graveyard
I was all by myself
When suddenly they woke
I wasn't alone
They were here
I needed to brawl all by myself
Then my arch-enemy appeared
Before my eyes
Blood dripped from his mammoth mouth
*Thud!*
A grave shook
Suddenly, the vampire's alabaster face
Stared at me,
I knew what I had to do,
I grabbed my knife and torch
'Woossshhh!'
A golden arrow hit me in the back
Of the neck...

**Shaun J Davidson (9)**
Flixton Junior School

# Dreamworld

**D** isaster and disorder, mischief and mayhem,

**R** oses wriggle and daisies dance,

**E** verything is not how you know it

**A** nts tower above magenta clouds like the morning mountains,

**M** ere it may sound,

**W** hen I can take you there,

**O** ver the sun, as cold as ice,

**R** oar! cry the people of the insect world, amidst the fleeing lions,

**L** ow underneath the bush of sweet, tongue-tantalising ice cream,

**D** ream and you will see the Dreamworld.

## Sophie Moorhouse (10)
Flixton Junior School

# Lost In Space

**L** ost and perplexed
**O** ut of reach of any help
**S** pace is like never-ending nothingness
**T** here's no gravity to put you right

**I** f I can't see which way is which
**N** ever will I find my way

**S** tars dance and spin
**P** lanets orbiting in circles
**A** mesmerising world
**C** omets crash and collide into a rocky surface
**E** xtremely ugly aliens jabbering to each other.

**Lizzie May Chapman (9)**
Flixton Junior School

# Spiders

**S** piders; why should you be afraid?
**P** eople mention that they shouldn't have been made
**I** f you saw a spider what would you do?
**D** on't stomp on it, just cry, 'Shoo!'
**E** ek, there's a spider in the house
**R** oaming around on the computer house
**S** o don't step on a spider whatever you do,

If you see a spider, just cry... 'Shoo!'

**Amelia Ashworth (9)**
Flixton Junior School

# A Nightmare In The Dark

**M** onsters everywhere, abnormally burly
**O** ne thousand of them glaring at me in the dingy, dark room
**N** ight terrors coming closer and closer
**S** tories say they slaughter in the dark
**T** he nests kept appearing they didn't halt
**E** verything around felt as hulking as space
**R** ight before it tried to eat me, I started to shriek and bellow
**S** uddenly, the door burst open and I perched up in my bed.

**Harrison Dow (10)**
Flixton Junior School

# The Monstrosity

My fear being tugged out of me
The monster of the night
It always brings a fright
Smoke covers the Earth with its hands
Time to run - *thud, thud, thud!*
The monsters have nearly reached me
*Roar* goes the monster with great menace
Like a lion that's had no food for days
I open my eyes to find I'm in my bed
It's all a dream, phew... I could have been dead.

**Elliot Ashcroft (10)**
Flixton Junior School

# Prehistoric Chase

I find myself in the jungle
but with two vicious raptors!
Their beady eyes glared at the trees,
causing them to quake.
Their scales shone amazingly
as they tempted one another for a bite.
Suddenly, one of the majestic birds
chomped on the body,
the other one pursued.
It sped along the mud as fast as a torpedo,
filled with rocket fuel,
with all the wind behind it, just for dinner...

**Toby Fletcher-Coleman (10)**
Flixton Junior School

# The Best Day Ever

One day
The best thing happened,
I could fly just like Peter Pan,
But I need to keep it a secret,
If I don't
Everyone will be asking me,
How do you do it?
Also when I swooped up to space,
It was magical and attractive,
It felt like my eyes would fall out,
It looked like a magical land,
Way better than that,
It was glorious and splendid.

**Oliver Hopewell (9)**
Flixton Junior School

# Darth Vader

There I was trapped by Darth Vader
He killed my best teammates.
With a swoosh of a lightsaber
Then all of a sudden the whole planet blew up
I saw orange sparkles spitting into the sky
The fire from the explosion was as hot as a volcano
As the ashes whooshed away, Darth Vader rose again.

**Joshua Smales (10)**
Flixton Junior School

# The Dragon

The dragon lives in a cave as dark as the beautiful
midnight sky
The dragon's fiery breath dances in the cave
*Whoosh!* The dragon flies away
The world disappears below him as he wakes up safe in
bed.

**Dan Bradshaw (9)**
Flixton Junior School

# Superpowers!

**S** ometimes I wonder what it's like to fly,
**U** nder the clouds, up, oh so high!
**P** retending to eat the clouds, mouth begins to drool,
**E** veryone starts to stare at me, they began to call me a fool.
**R** iding on the stars, swimming through the sun
**P** lease don't stop, never-ending fun!
**O** h we can't let them bully us
**W** e must get them back!
**E** veryone looking at me in a strange way
**R** eally, I don't know why!
**S** uddenly, I realise that I can fly!

**Felicia Connolly**
St Bernard's RC Primary School

# Mythical Masterpiece

I'm on a journey to the moon
I hope I get there soon
I see Abraham Lincoln the unicorn
With about 1000 horns.

Ecstatic, flattered, I laid down in my luxurious bed
Whilst Chef Shakespeare is cooking for
everyone needed to be fed.
Shakespeare the butler,
Writing stories while cooking with butter.

'This bus has got talent,' says Dec
'Not as much as me,' says Ant.
'Our boat is drowning all hands on deck!'
'It must have been caused by an ant!'

The moon isn't far away now
What I ask is how?
The mission was expected to fail
That was when it started to hail.
'Mission abort!'

**Damon Norman Marley Wilson (10)**
St James CE Primary School

# A Magical Land

I once met a unicorn,
In a magical land,
Who was very kind and helpful,
And led a perfect hand.

I had then seen its horn glitter,
In the bright light,
Although it's dark and hard to see,
It glitters in the night
The unicorn in a rainbow,
Showing off itself,
Even though it runs everywhere,
It has a lot of health.

We were trying to find a Pegasus and Griffin
The rarest creatures ever,
And if you know they are close by,
They will drop a soft feather.

We were on our way until,
A fairy said hello,
Whose wings glittered like the sun
And shimmered a nice yellow.

Suddenly, we heard a sound
Coming from a large rock,
And surprisingly the creatures were near,
A dock!

We took the creatures home,
And fed them with joy,
And we then realised,
We were not alone...

**Mia Blackburn (10)**
St James CE Primary School

# Tick~Tock

Where am I
Why am I doing a test?
It is obvious I am not the best!

What am I going to do?
I haven't studied yet!
My score is obviously going to be zero
Which everyone bets (even my friends)

Frightened, terrified, exhausted I feel like I'm going to burn
Even if cheating is wrong
Therefore, I need to turn.

But what is that band doing on my wrist
Connected to it is a piece of paper
With a list?

It says, 'Clap once and you will be amazed.'
Therefore I clapped once and looked around as I gazed...

**Junior Mbaru (10)**
St James CE Primary School

# Killer Toast

The brown smothered toast started to throw
marshmallows at me
So I smothered it with tea.
I stuffed it full with butter, tea and
melted marshmallow,
Then it exploded.
Sadly it made a hole then it formed back together.
I threw a shiny, just washed spoon at it and it still
survived.
Then I made it fall into a spiky pit.
Someone (Bob) wanted to buy it.
When he bought it, I killed it by taking a bite!

**Dylan William Statham (10)**
St James CE Primary School

# Hogwarts

**H** ow to do spells, wizardry and sorcery
**O** ld as a tortoise and a beard white as snow
**G** o to Hogwarts and learn
**W** ill spells be easy or hard to do?
**A** s colossal as skyscrapers
**R** ead a lot of spell books
**T** ry to do tricky sorcery
**S** ee Harry Potter and Dumbledore.

**Cayden France (10)**
St James CE Primary School

# Man Of The Match

Manchester Dragons are my favourite team
I went to watch them play football and I got pulled in
by the manager
And they asked me to play,
After the match they gave me a trial for the team
Then lots of other teams came in.
They wanted to get me to play for them.
'Never!' I said, 'I will not play for any other team
I want to play for Manchester Dragons.'
On the other side of the team stadium was a ball,
All I had to do was score a goal. I ran over to the ball
And scored an amazing goal.
Finally I got a place on the team, I was delighted.

The next day I went to play a match
And I was Man of the Match!
'Man of the Match,' my dad said,
'You're already doing good.'
At training I was in the first team and I became
famous.

The next match was amazing,
I was scoring lots of goals
'Cheating!' one of the other team said to me
Because we had won, but I was not!

**Alfie Atkinson (8)**
St Margaret Mary's RC Primary School

# The Amazing Superhero

**T** hink again and take that man back to prison where he belongs

**H** eat filling me with my surroundings

**E** nergy is getting sucked from my body from all the poisonous animals biting me

**S** uperheroes flying and beating everyone off through the sky

**U** ltimately sad from all the disaster that is happening

**P** etrified villains run away from all the heroes

**E** cstatic about what has jut been mastered, I go up to the villains to give them a massive punch

**R** elieved of them not coming back again, I walk away

**H** eroes high five each other as victory occurs again

**E** veryone sees our greatness and knows we are a good team

**R** oaring cheers and happy people

**O** h, see them as they fly through the sky!

**Joshua Solomon (10)**
St Margaret Mary's RC Primary School

# Creepy Night Fear

**C** reeping up in the night
**R** eaching out to scare in the darkness
**E** nclosed by the fear
**E** scape the frightening face of the monster
**P** eeking silently to grab something
**Y** earning to scare upon the young.

**N** ightmare becomes a reality
**I** gnore the silence of the darkness
**G** littering of the moonlight
**H** overing anxiously around the room
**T** aking souls from each house

**F** ur as rough as sandpaper
**E** erie glasses smashing in front of the bed
**A** wful noises of scraping
**R** oaring to scare upon people.

**Mili Gibson (11)**
St Margaret Mary's RC Primary School

# Once Upon A Dream

I dreamt that I was in a candy house,
Chocolate birds were tweeting and washing in the
chocolate fountain
As a cookie cat chased the toffee mice around the
garden.
Strolling along the candy cane path.
I saw candyfloss trees.
Growing beside the liquorice grass.
Then a swirly candy cow came along and let me milk
him.
I loved it!
Then I carried on skipping along on the candy cane
paths.
I went back to the candy house and chomped on the
candy mixed all together
It was good, yum!
So I woke up, I was amazed with swirls around my
head!

**Layla O'Malley (7)**
St Margaret Mary's RC Primary School

# Turning A Professional Skateboarder

**S** weating but still going and still happy
**K** eep on going till you land the trick
**A** lways stay focused and stay calm
**T** ake turns and don't go when it is someone else's go
**E** xcited to wake up in the morning
**B** uy a new skateboard when yours breaks badly
**O** ak is used to make skateboards
**A** lways go for the trick, every time!
**R** un with the skateboard to get speed
**D** on't get frustrated
**E** at to get energy to skate
**R** ide the skateboard every day to get better.

**Charlie Lomas (7)**
St Margaret Mary's RC Primary School

# Where Have You Gone, Miss Unicorn?

Where have you gone, Miss Unicorn?
You were here the other night,
I'm getting into a fright,
Now the sun has gone to sleep
And the moon is wide awake.

You should be here tonight
I will not be able to go to a dream
Which is far away
Without you, I'm scared.

This is not meant to be,
Hurry, hurry Miss Unicorn, before I'm wide awake,
I want to see you tonight,
There you are, Miss Unicorn, now it's time to sleep
To run away to my little midnight dream.

**Savannah-Rose Gethin (10)**
St Margaret Mary's RC Primary School

# Beautiful Butterflies!

Oh butterflies, you are so beautiful
Lying on my bed I can see you
Twirling around like a cradle
Please don't leave me, you are my only friend
Your beautiful colours make me relaxed
Watching you land in your nests, you make me fall
asleep
Stars on the wall and you bringing them down to me
My dog is with everyone snuggling up together
Landing on the canopy, you're watching me and I
am watching you
You're making me happy, oh, oh my,
What will I do without you,
When you fly away?

**Elliah Caine (10)**
St Margaret Mary's RC Primary School

# Nightmares With Fairies

Come back, fairest fairy
I know you've been stolen
I know you've been captured
I know you're not in a bed full of gold.
I could notice you from afar with that blue swishy hair
See your wings with colours as spotty as a cheetah.
My worries all go.
I have found you and will take you back to your Fairy
Land.
I will be the saviour.
I will be the hero.
Don't worry about your worries.
You've got the fairest fairy of them all to cover all
those nightmare dreams.

**Ruby Bates-Clarke (9)**
St Margaret Mary's RC Primary School

# Victory Doesn't Come Without Sacrifice

Victory's sweet but it's not easy, war is life-changing
But within it, holds great sacrifice
But great sacrifice doesn't come without risk and
honour.

Come back soldier, we haven't won yet
We run through misty smoke that really gave me poke
Your large army and big guns can be seen from a year
away,
Let me charge forward and get this win.

Our life depends on this, we shall not give a fright
But we must be willing to put up a fight for our right.

**Cain Wildbure (10)**
St Margaret Mary's RC Primary School

# I Miss You

Every day I think of you
You're all I've ever known and knew,
Nothing I have compares to you,
Every day I think of you.

Even though you're up in the sky,
At this age I still cry,
About the day you went up, up and away,
I still have a million reasons why
You should have stayed.

Why did you go, ever so soon?
I thought I was the beat and you were the tune,
To my broken heart you were the screw...

I miss you.

**Tomisin Comfort Olutayo (10)**
St Margaret Mary's RC Primary School

# The Faraway

To find what you seek, you must go slow,
But make the wrong step and the spiders will show!
This all started deep, deep in a cave,
Where the spiders took me, me as a slave.
Red eyes staring deep in your soul,
They never stop, unless they're climbing a pole.
Spiders here, spiders there, spiders everywhere,
All they want to see is your blood right there...
To find what you seek you must go slow,
But make the wrong step and the spiders will show!

**Kevin Kusmierek (11)**
St Margaret Mary's RC Primary School

# Wonderful Witches

I am a witch
Soaring through the sky
The black cat is called Kate
Behind me on the broom.

She is a black cat
Who likes to chase a rat
She made me fly to the moon
On purpose because she wanted
To be on the moon.

Then we were on the moon
A bright, white moon
That shines as bright
As the sun.

They built a giant magic castle there
It was as big as a skyscraper
It had gardens and everything
Even a pool!

**Jessica Fairchild (8)**
St Margaret Mary's RC Primary School

# Night, Night...

**N** ight... night... don't let the bed bugs bite...
**I** hope you sleep tight...
**G** ulp... gulp...
**H** a ha ha...
**T** urn around...

**N** ow the future was up to me...
**I** said to myself...
**G** et out of here!
**H** e followed me...
**T** o the place...

**S** creaming and crying whilst I paced
**O** n the door a rope stood, hanging...
**'N** o,' I screamed, as I didn't want hanging...

## Alex Lomas (11)
St Margaret Mary's RC Primary School

# Funland

When I go to Funland the waves *swish* and *swoosh*.
My friends, the elves, love to play
On the forever bubbles that *swish* and *sway.*
Instead of rain, every wish I've ever dreamt falls down.
So it swishes and sways all day long
It never stops
Until you sing a song.
Your dream will come true in Funland.
When the elves click their fingers you zoom around
Until you get to the moon.
*Zoom, zoom, zoom!*

**Mia Nolan (8)**
St Margaret Mary's RC Primary School

# Famous Singer

I am really nervous,
Like I have never been before.
I also feel a bit anxious,
I feel like I'm in a peach's core.

I am with my cat though
I am going to sing so,
Lalalalalalala,
Then a baby at my concert says, 'Ba ba.'

The crowd goes wild,
I feel excited,
Everyone is cheering for one mile
I hope my family is very ecstatic.

My manager is proud
My cat has prowled,
How lucky I feel.

**Emma Jenkins-Meehan (7)**
St Margaret Mary's RC Primary School

# Candy World

As I drifted into a dream
I saw someone who I didn't know
I was curious.

I went over then I stumbled into some melted
chocolate mud
It looked delicious.

When I got to the marshmallows
Someone was bouncing around them
They were having fun
I joined in, yippee!

I said, 'Hi.'
She replied, 'Hi. What's your name?'
I replied, 'Caitlin, what's yours?'
'Ella.'

**Caitlin Marie Burrows (9)**
St Margaret Mary's RC Primary School

# Who Is It?

Who is that, a man, a woman, an animal?
An object stood there alone in my closet
Where is it off to? Where has it gone?
Off to a land of wild and fun?
Shall I follow, shall I stay?
But if I do I might not come back.
Well, that's not a high chance.
So I follow and say, 'Hey! Stop there, what do you look like, why are you full of hair?'
It turns around and all I see is me full of anger, full of hate.
It's time for me to change my ways.

**Luca Daniel Robertson (10)**
St Margaret Mary's RC Primary School

# My Mermaid Dream

As my mind drifted, I felt myself turning into a
beautiful mermaid.
Swimming along the sea, types of different fish I saw,
sharks and starfish
And other sea animals.
Then I met one of the other mermaids called Jennifer,
She looked nice.
I started following her but something happened
Magical glowing and glimmering sparks were all over
me.
I was transforming again,
I was pulled out of the water and I was safe back home
in bed.

**Angel Owa (8)**
St Margaret Mary's RC Primary School

# Clowns In The Air!

**N** ightmares have been prepared for you
**I** n your petrifying dream, red eyes will gleam
**G** leaming scary clowns leaning behind trees!
**H** ealing scars on the face like ours
**T** ime is ticking for them to come out
**M** oon shining on the red nose,
**A** rms as white as can be
**R** ed curly hair twisted and twirly,
**E** erie voices like a mouse all over the universe
**S** pooky eyes when clowns lie.

**Remi Smith (9)**
St Margaret Mary's RC Primary School

# Monsters

**M** urdering innocent children while they dream of candy canes,

**O** n their tiptoes, they ruthlessly hunt the ruby-red blood

**N** ever thinking twice about the consequences that await

**S** lurping the sweet blood like a milkshake

**T** rying to stop the murderous ways

**E** ven though it hurts me to say - they will never stop!

**R** elentless, relentless

**S** orry children, they're behind you!

**Lacey Inman (11)**
St Margaret Mary's RC Primary School

# The Corridor

Trapped in an endless corridor,
With infinite amounts of doors.
As I near the first handle
I get a feeling of warmth like that of a candle.

I open the door and see, my hopes too
My hopes to have a family.
Then I feel pulled towards,
The door for no cowards.

I feel the burning sensation of a flame,
As the door opens to my bane.
Light flashes through my eyes,
I'm dancing with such terrible lies.

**Gabriel Downes (11)**
St Margaret Mary's RC Primary School

# Once Upon A Dreamland

Lying in my cosy bed,
I felt my imagination swiftly drift away into Dreamland.
As I bounced along the bumpy road of ice cream,
Lollipops greeted me happily.
I walked up to a cherry blossom tree,
And saw a girl, she smiled at me.
We played all day long.
I said goodbye and left.

I saw golden humming birds,
Singing like angels.
I slept in a cosy chocolate home,
But woke up at home.

**Jennifer Otame (8)**
St Margaret Mary's RC Primary School

# Up In Space

As I stepped into the training
I really wasn't complaining,
To see all the different faces,
Separated out like mazes.

It took forever to get to space,
But it wasn't at all put to waste,
In the rocket I got to fly,
Oh no, I think I'm going to be sick
Because it is so high!
3
2
1, blast-off!

It really was so bright,
Up in the dark space night,
Being the first woman on the moon!

**Mikayla Ocheja (10)**
St Margaret Mary's RC Primary School

# Zero Zone

A hallway full of mysteries,
It's old now and it's history.
Zero Zone is the best
Zero Zone never rests.

Voices are always speaking
The little drainpipes are probably leaking
This is Zero Zone
We don't have phones.

Or flying drones.
Is Zero Zone actually real?
Is someone writing about Zero Zone?
The walls are turning red.

Aah! Wait, I can't believe it, I'm in my bed.

**Joel Lynch (10)**
St Margaret Mary's RC Primary School

# The Amazing Features Of A Plant

The inside of a plant is where the bee buzzes.
When it is ready it goes back to the hive and feeds the
cute baby bees
How amazing is that?
When I am gardening I feel glorious and free.
The plants have senses just like us
But not all senses, just taste, feel, touch.
You remember the seven life processes.
I have seventy-four plants.
How busy we were!
Me and my family planted four each day.

**Brooke Taylor (7)**
St Margaret Mary's RC Primary School

# Sweets And Chocolate

I was going into a different world,
I saw a football pitch,
It was made out of sweets and chocolate.
I was amazed!
I had never seen anything like this before,
I started to play football,
I wanted to get the shiny cup.
It was as shiny as gold.
The cup was made out of yellow icing.
The football was made out of black and white icing,
I was amazed!

**Olivia Blackwell (9)**
St Margaret Mary's RC Primary School

# Mischief Monsters

**M** onsters will always give you a fright

**O** h, also make sure you hold the covers tight...

**N** othing is going to prepare me for what I'm about to see

**S** o now I better go and flee

**T** hud! Something moves, it's creeping around

**E** yes glow like a bright glow-worm

**R** eady for fright, it jumps out on me

**S** uddenly, I wake up in my bed.

## Ella-Rose Taylor-Dolan (8)

St Margaret Mary's RC Primary School

# he Warrior

When I close my eyes
And drift to sleep
I leave my body,
And my mind runs free.
This enables me to become
Lily the Warrior.

My trusty horse will lead me there,
When we travel the world,
And stop the depression,
Join who agrees
But explain to others who don't

I'm clumsy,
Stubborn
But I stand up for others
And that is a true warrior!

**Jennifer Dayo Ogunjobi (10)**
St Margaret Mary's RC Primary School

# Robots

Once upon a dream
I was walking down the street with shiny,
glimmering robots
When I was at my house
Two men were riding horses
And a man was on a carriage which was glowing.
The horses could fly.
The horses flew as high as a plane,
They made rainbows and flew to the moon.
When they were coming down
They did the loop-the-loop
And then they flew down with a safe landing.

**Jayden Barnes (8)**
St Margaret Mary's RC Primary School

# Super Dragon And Louis The Dragon Wizard

I dreamt I was bitten by a spider
And turned to a dragon.
I flew into a room like a giant's room.
It was like a giant's egg.
There was a dragon dressed up as a hero.
He flew towards me and said, 'Are you alright after that big fall?'
I said, 'What? I flew through the entrance'
He said, 'There's no exit, or is there?'
Then the dream ended.

**Louis (9)**
St Margaret Mary's RC Primary School

# Fluttering Fairies

Once upon a dream in a festive world,
The fluttering fairies twinkle multicoloured
Glows in the candyfloss like clouds

The rainbow waterfall is in the centre
Of the misty, murky forest.

The colossal chocolate trees -
Encased with luscious marshmallows -
Make your mouth melt away.
This is where the reality of dreams is made...

**Shondrella Gachoka (11)**
St Margaret Mary's RC Primary School

# Unicorns

**U** nusual unicorns flying across the universe
**N** oisy unicorns singing very loud
**I** ntelligent unicorns answering questions
**C** uddly unicorns hugging children
**O** ozy unicorns messing the place up
**R** ushing unicorns doing a Race for Life
**N** ice unicorns playing happily
**S** leepy unicorns having naps.

**Thomas Hulston (7)**
St Margaret Mary's RC Primary School

# Candy Land

**C** andy Land is my home now
**A** s sweetness touches my tongue (I love it)
**N** utritious sweets spring past me
**D** ark chocolate climbs my nose
**Y** our hands touch the candyfloss

**L** ines of gingerbread men
**A** s well as gingerbread girls
**N** ew flavours start to hatch
**D** ancing chocolate trains *choo choo* on.

**Iliana Dimitropoulou (10)**
St Margaret Mary's RC Primary School

# The Chocolate World

As I drifted into a dream
The floor began to change into a river of chocolate.
I touched the ground, it was gooey and messy.
The rain was tasty candy.
Suddenly, I started to fly, it was such a sight.

I was so amazed that I was in the toffee sky.
As I flew in the toffee sky, I only found a chocolate flat.
I felt happy and free.

**Joseph Tattersall (9)**
St Margaret Mary's RC Primary School

# Once Upon A Time

Once upon a time,
I was a lonely girl,
Trying to chase my dreams,
I hope I will retrieve them.

Once upon a time,
I was on the verge of death,
The worst time not the best,
I was being put to the test.

Once upon a time,
I was alone and stuck,
It was dark and dismal,
For I was out of luck.

**Erin Bennett (10)**
St Margaret Mary's RC Primary School

# Football Dreams

**F** ootballs flying in all directions, en route to the World Cup Final

**O** verhead, footballs fly in the sky.

**O** ver there is where to go!

**T** o Planet Earth, to the match

**B** ut space and Earth are not connected

**A** lot of balls start to guide me

**L** ots of them!

**L** ast I make the Final of the World Cup.

**Liam Mcculloch (10)**
St Margaret Mary's RC Primary School

# Angel Wings

**A** ngel wings fly me to the sky
**N** ever fail you
**G** et you when you fall
**E** very day I fly to school
**L** onger than 7ft long.

**W** ings that fly you sky-high
**I** never thought it could happen
**N** ever knew I could
**G** et to fly with you
**S** till by your side.

**Liberty Thompson (10)**
St Margaret Mary's RC Primary School

# Pirates Save The Day

Pirates come to save as many people as possible.
I got saved and had a long and good journey across the sea.
Raiders tried to attack innocent people
Then that was when the pirates came along to save the day.
At that moment a huge cannonball shot
and scared them away.
Treasure was found where 'X' marks the spot.

**Liam Kearney (8)**
St Margaret Mary's RC Primary School

# The Greatest Team

In a land far... far... away
I was a footballer, a really famous one.
I was with my friends and we were looking for a
team to face.
As soon as we conceded a goal
We faced them and if they won they could destroy the
Earth!
If we won, we could keep the Earth and destroy them...
We won 6-5.
Fifty years later, they came back.

**Thomas Leggat (8)**
St Margaret Mary's RC Primary School

# Flying To The Moon

Lying in my bed hugging my teddy, Fred
I discovered I was in a land so pretty and grand
I stopped at a flying bus, the wind blew and went
*whoosh!*
It went on the moon, it was more than soon
On the moon we jumped so high
Then I opened my eyes
Out my bedroom window all I could spy
Was the night sky.

**Sienna Kelly (8)**
St Margaret Mary's RC Primary School

# The Beam Of My Dream

When I get to bed
And lay down my head.
I had a weird dream
Along this theme I gained powers
Whilst my friend grew flowers.
I fought bad guys
And ate pies
I wished this dream would never end
But I did for me and my friend.
'Wake up!' my dad did scream
And that was the beam of my dream.

**George Francis Partington (9)**
St Margaret Mary's RC Primary School

# Football Dreams

Footballs flying in the air,
Oh I just don't care.

As it lands near the stadium
I wonder why it's there.

As I go in the stadium,
I feel special.

I start playing,
It is so amazing.

My journey has been wonderful,
I just hope it doesn't end.

**Tom Fauguel (10)**
St Margaret Mary's RC Primary School

# Dream Come True

Sitting on the chair in the shop called Frashion
I was doing a beautiful, colourful dress for a girl.
She had blue eyes like the sky.
She was going to a birthday party.
When I finished the girl came.
She had a beautiful hairstyle like a princess.
The dress' fan was colourful as an ocean.

**Wiktoria Pietras (8)**
St Margaret Mary's RC Primary School

# Nightmare

Once I saw something in the darkness,
Glowing and shining near.
So eager to find out, I was in so much fear.

It was coming closer and closer,
I didn't know what to do,
Trying to find a way out, and a lever too.

Finally I woke up in bed,
The dream was gone from my head.

**Alex Cooke (9)**
St Margaret Mary's RC Primary School

# Famous Teacher

**T** oday the teacher will be teaching
**E** verybody enjoys the teacher teaching
**A** teacher can be famous like Taylor Swift
**C** atching the pencil, I began to lift
**H** elping my friend, I sniff...
**E** njoy playtime and learning
**R** unning through the field, playing fairly.

**Katie Ann Dean (10)**
St Margaret Mary's RC Primary School

# Police Lady

Sitting on the sofa, I dreamt about being a police lady.
I would be brave and I would fight crimes.

I would fight crimes and stop bad people.
I would be kind.

I would fight naughty people and love others
Who tell the truth.

Then I was going into the police station.

**Bailey Reese Downes (8)**
St Margaret Mary's RC Primary School

# Ronald

**R** onald McDonald is famous for fast food

**O** h Ronald McDonald, you are my favourite dude

**N** inja McDonald at your red-haired service

**A** technology expert like Ronald cannot make a burger

**L** and of his hand can make you into a joker

**D** onald is like a lurker.

## Michael-Joe Creilly (10)
St Margaret Mary's RC Primary School

# The Clumsy Clown

I was walking in the park when suddenly a clown came running
And a terrible teacher came running after him.
The clown picked me up and carried me to hide.
When the teacher had gone, we went to his house.
The clown said, 'Stay here, whilst I go and save more people.'

**Hayden Scott Lindley (8)**
St Margaret Mary's RC Primary School

# Chased Down

**C** hased down
**H** eavily breathing
**A** nightmare overwhelmed me
**S** harp turns
**E** vading the trees
**D** eath plagued my mind

**D** own to the cellar
**O** ver the pipes
**W** ater all around me
**N** o one in sight...

**Oliver Anthony Steven Newman (10)**
St Margaret Mary's RC Primary School

# Fun House

**F** ear is in the air
**U** nicorns are nowhere to be seen
**N** o one's helping me
**H** e is just around the corner
**O** h no, it's a clown
**U** nderneath the floorboards are screams
**S** afe house, more like fun house!
**E** scape fast!

**Libbie Gerzsei (10)**
St Margaret Mary's RC Primary School

# Final

**F** ootball is the best
**I** 'm a United player
**N** ot a City player
**A** lso I like Athletico Madrid
**L** et's go and impress some football fans

This is what I dream of each night,
I dream and hope with all my might.

**Aiden Leggat (10)**
St Margaret Mary's RC Primary School

# The Imaginary World

As I walk along the trees,
I feel the wind hit me
Like a fearsome, cold ice cube.

As I walk across the branches
I see a colourful rainbow.
I jump onto it and then I smell toffee
I walk across the branches
And then I eat the toffee.

**Leighton Woodlock (9)**
St Margaret Mary's RC Primary School

# Once Upon A Dream

I pushed myself out of bed.
I thought to myself that I should get some apples off
the tree
So I raced out the door.
Butterflies danced around my feet and the birds sang
to me.
The wind threw itself at me
As I strolled back to my candy cottage.

**Lois Bennett (8)**
St Margaret Mary's RC Primary School

# Dragons

**D** ragons zooming around
**R** acing and playing
**A** round the stars
**G** iggling and laughing
**O** n a moving planet
**N** othing to be seen except beautiful stars and planets floating in the sea that is space.

## Max Middleton (10)
St Margaret Mary's RC Primary School

# Meet Someone Famous

**G** o to America and you will see
**R** ound the bend is another bend
**A** riana is a singer
**N** ow she's in concert, she will have a sore finger
**D** ancing on stage
**E** very time she's about to fade.

**Laykia Bell (9)**
St Margaret Mary's RC Primary School

# Candy World

Lying in bed, I suddenly drifted into an imaginary world
The ground was made out of sparkling shining sweets,
Like the sun glinting on the cyan river.
My bed was a marshmallow,
As I lay down on my bed,
I sank into it.

**Joseph Bailey (8)**
St Margaret Mary's RC Primary School

# Spider Tales

Spider, spider, where could you be?
Webbing the roof? Webbing the side?
What are you doing?
When can I see you?
What should I do?
I am waiting for you.
When can I see you?
Why can't I see you now?

**Daniel Trotter (10)**
St Margaret Mary's RC Primary School

# Famous

Being famous is very shameless,
You get to sign people's autographs,
I have lots of photographs,
It makes people feel happy
According to Maddie,
That's why famous is so shameless.

**Mia Pandolfo (10)**
St Margaret Mary's RC Primary School

# Lost Forest

A
Lost forest
In the middle
Of nowhere. There's
A map in the
Middle of nowhere
Find it and be
Awesome at everything
The
Map
In
The
Middle
Of
No
Where.

### Scola Wakomo (7)
St Margaret Mary's RC Primary School

# Dreams

**D** reams are good,
**R** un from all nightmares.
**E** at anything you like,
**A** nything you want can be accomplished,
**M** e and you now know everything about dreams.

**Benjamin Blackwell (11)**
St Margaret Mary's RC Primary School

# Billie

**B** eautifully kind
**I** n an imaginary mind
**L** ovely as can be
**L** ucky is she
**I** keep her close in my dreams
**E** ven when I'm eating beans.

**Kiera Doyle (10)**
St Margaret Mary's RC Primary School

# My Dream

The bright sky was shining through my window,
It was as light as the lamp
And obviously bigger than my Nintendo.
My house was big and red.
I was excited to get out of my bed.
I took my first step,
And felt like I was dead.
My arms and legs couldn't move,
They were as heavy as lead.
Suddenly, I realised I was in a cage.
A wizard appeared, he was twelve times my age.
Then he said, 'So you've woken up have you?'
'Yes I have, but my hands and legs are poo.'
'I know, you have stayed there for sixty weeks.'
'Really? I never realised that many weeks.'
'It is World War 3,'
'But there are no bombs, it surely cannot be.'
Then a bomb came through the roof
Suddenly I woke up, Tom my dad and Lillie my mum
Would definitely not believe my dream.

**Paul Connolly (9)**
St Mary's RC Primary School

# I Had A Dream

I had a dream I was playing football with
Real Madrid

H aving a team talk with them, I'm number 8
A moment later we were going to the tunnel
D o I dare wake up? No, I shouldn't

A ll the Barcelona players were there

D ani Carvajal said, 'Good luck.'
R efs were there, it was time, I was as scared as a bee
in rain
E veryone was shouting my name
A fter that, we were walking out
M y dream was over, what an amazing night.

**Samuel Kane**
St Mary's RC Primary School

# Candy World

**C** andy World is great, you should come
**A** ny time, you'd better fill your tum.
**N** o one leaves, it's the place of your dreams
**D** ouble Deckers are as sweet as watermelons
**Y** ummy sweets as big as lemons.

**W** orld you have never seen before
**O** thers want to lick the door
**R** ain is sugar drops
**L** oads of sweets just for you
**D** id you know cows do candy poo?

**Leon Lebeter (9)**
St Mary's RC Primary School

# I'm Going To Candy Land

Today I woke up and I'm in Candy Land
I go downstairs and see a cupcake trampoline
I see my friends down the street
And they're eating candy, mmm.

I like candy a lot so I join in with them
The chocolate is melting like a snowman in the sun
I see a button and I press it,
The world goes upside down.

I stumble a little bit,
I wake up and see it was only a dream
That happened to me.

**Samantha Sheldon (8)**
St Mary's RC Primary School

# Adventure Land

I zoom past the sun, it is as red as a ruby
I pass the forest into the abyss.

I start to think of a plan
To get away from this man.

And till then I will proceed
Then I will start to read.

The forest is dark
Then I see sparkles next to the park

I fly to the heroic monsters
Then I start greeting.

I am sneaking past them all
Then I started to fall...

**Michael Sunmola**
St Mary's RC Primary School

# Scary Audition

I said bye to Mum
I gave Leah a hug
Then they wished me luck as I wandered in
I shouted, 'I am here!'
Then I saw something run,
I thought I was dumb.

I opened the door
Something was there for sure
I turned around, it was a monster with a very poor
claw.
The next minute I was upside down.
I am flying out the window,
My mum and I have turned into monsters,
But nice monsters.

**Grace Wakefield Chinnery (9)**
St Mary's RC Primary School

# Lost

It was a day like no other
Famous flying teachers with superpowers.

Suddenly, *bang! Crackle!*
I was awoken by dragons

*Bang!* Suddenly, I was in a different world
Every town and country were unknown
The park was made of bark
Three-eyed weird people are all around
The journey is coming to an end
I'm as sad as Mona Lisa. The bus has gone...

**Sofia Da Silva (9)**
St Mary's RC Primary School

# Unicorn, Mr Unicorn

**M** r Unicorn is kind and full of joy
**R** ealising who Mr Unicorn is, is a big moment

**U** nicorns are kind but dangerous too
**N** ine unicorns die a year
**I** will save unicorns with Jaz and Munch
**C** oral Reef is a unicorn palace in the sea
**O** nly a unicorn can enter
**R** arely the palace is closed
**N** ice unicorns eat fairy dust.

**Kiera Fortune (9)**
St Mary's RC Primary School

# Fairies!

There is a land that nobody knows
It is where imaginations grow
There are tiny houses
As small as mouses.

There are other fairies fluttering in the sky
It is where fairy tales lie
You will hear rivers,
It will never give you a shiver.

The other fairies are very kind
There is nothing to hide,
I am the sugar fairy!
We can defeat the scary!

**Nancy Wilson**
St Mary's RC Primary School

# Car Land

Now I'm at Car Land
A Mercedes meets me at the gate
Ronaldo, Rooney and David Beckham
We jump in the Mercedes
And off we go!

When the journey finishes
We get in a new car
Ranger flashes his lights
We get in the car and
Off we go!

The journey has nearly finished
But it has not
Tesla flashes his lights
We get in the car and
Off we go!

**Ruairi Nisbet**
St Mary's RC Primary School

# My Secret Fairy

I have a secret fairy
She is as happy as can be
I have a secret fairy
To me she smiles with glee.

I have a secret fairy
She is so beautiful
I have a secret fairy
She is never not fun

I have a secret fairy
She can fly so high
I have a secret fairy
She flies up, up to the sky.

**Freya Grace Rothwell (9)**
St Mary's RC Primary School

# Miss Agnew

**M** iss Agnew
**I** s nice
**S** he is very helpful
**S** he's a very good teacher

**A** s good as a parent
**G** ood at very hard work
**N** ew homework for kids
**E** ven helps the very naughty people for
**W** ork and is the best teacher in the world.

## Dave Anil (9)
St Mary's RC Primary School

# My Secret Unicorn

I have a secret unicorn
She is happy as can be
I have this dream she
Takes me to the galaxy.

We are flying high in the sky
In the day we bounce
On the fluffy clouds

At night we look
At the beautiful stars
Shining bright like
Diamonds.

**Vesta Balseviciute (9)**
St Mary's RC Primary School

# I See You Everywhere

**L** ovely as a unicorn
**O** ften I see you but you're in the lounge
**V** olcanoes blast into space and I see your face
**E** xperiments are great, better than tying your lace
**L** earning is great, like meat with heat
**Y** o-yos are fun, like eating a bun.

## Munachi Unagha (9)
St Mary's RC Primary School

# Super Unicorn

There was a super unicorn
Flying through the air
Her wings were like butterflies
Fluttering in the breeze
The beautiful smile upon her face
Spreads like melted chocolate all over the place
This super unicorn was my best friend forever.

**Jazmyne-Antonia Devon Corbishley (8)**
St Mary's RC Primary School

# Getting Lost

A famous actor getting lost drives a boat to get back
home.
Runs into a whirlpool
And falls into a sewer.
Finds another actor so they travelled together.
They walked for days and they finally didn't make it.
They ended up in a bad dream.

**Kaven Shepley (9)**
St Mary's RC Primary School

# Magic Land

**M** ake a wish and you will see
**A** magical fairy as cute as can be
**G** alloping along magical unicorns is all you can see
**I** n the sky smiles are glee,
**C** ome and join me in Magic Land.

**Ben Kahraman (9)**
St Mary's RC Primary School

# The Magic Kingdom

One magical crystal falls and all outside is candy
There are genies flying in mid-air
You only have three wishes
An icy sea on the beach
I jump on the top of the water
It has sparkles on top
I discover that... I can breathe under the water.

**Alex Cardus (6)**
St Michael's CE Primary School

# I Wish

I wish I had a crown
I wish I was a princess
I wish I had a castle
In my lovely dream.

I wish I had a dolphin
I wish I could ride a whale
I wish I could swim in the deep blue ocean
In my lovely dream.

**Charlotte Suzanne Redfern (7)**
St Michael's CE Primary School

# The Gold Land

In my dream there are lots of gold cars
My tummy is tickling
I am going faster than an aeroplane
I'm going 6000,00000,0000 miles per hour
I'm racing through boggy mud
I'm driving up a muddy hill.

**Nathaniel Jacobs (7)**
St Michael's CE Primary School

# The Magic Mansion

I wish I lived in a mansion that is made of sweets
Inside the door is made of gold
The lamp is made of solid gold
It's so beautiful you can't even look at it
In my mansion I will roller-skate.

**Violetta Farrington (7)**
St Michael's CE Primary School

# The Dragon And Me

I can see a palace with crystals all over it
Inside the palace I have a pet dragon
And a magic wizard
I have superpowers
I am a famous footballer.

**Carter Burgess (7)**
St Michael's CE Primary School

# My Dream

**P** laying with great friends
**A** lways playing on the swings
**R** iding a horse like a jockey
**K** icking a ball high up in the blue sky.

**Will David Thompson (7)**
St Michael's CE Primary School

# Into The Woods We Go

Scary and you can hear the branches falling
I can see an extraordinary, yellow small door
I smell a whiff of bark
We can play and climb trees.

**Leo-Alan Sparkes (6)**
St Michael's CE Primary School

# The Chocolate Palace

I live in a huge chocolate palace
With a chocolate river
And a chocolate waterfall
If I eat anything
It will come back again.

**Archie Ryan Kilroy (7)**
St Michael's CE Primary School

# Untitled

I live in an ice cream house
It has got chocolate floors
And bubblegum doors
And strawberry walls.
Wait till you taste.

**Evan Lewis Vines (7)**
St Michael's CE Primary School

# The Marshmallow World

I live in a marshmallow palace
My palace is pink and white.
It's full of joy.
You will see a world of happiness and laughter.

**Sienna Hannah Hostey (7)**
St Michael's CE Primary School

# The Candy Land

I saw a candy shop
I got a pop
I went home and ate the cone
I went to dance and prance.

**Georgina Davies (7)**
St Michael's CE Primary School

YoungWriters
Est.1991

# YOUNG WRITERS
# INFORMATION

We hope you have enjoyed reading this book – and
that you will continue to in the coming years.

If you're a young writer who enjoys reading and creative writing,
or the parent of an enthusiastic poet or story writer,
do visit our website **www.youngwriters.co.uk**. Here you will
find free competitions, workshops and games, as well as
recommended reads, a poetry glossary and our blog.

If you would like to order further copies of this book,
or any of our other titles, then please give us a
call or visit **www.youngwriters.co.uk**.

Young Writers
Remus House
Coltsfoot Drive
Peterborough
PE2 9BF
(01733) 890066
info@youngwriters.co.uk